# POETICALLY CORRECT

### BY

## QUENTIN M. CODDING

1st BOOKS LIBRARY
Bloomington, Indiana

ISBN: 0-75963-319-3

This book is printed on acid free paper.

1stBooks - rev. 10/15/01

# CONTENTS

PAGE


Preface .................................................................................... vii
YOU'RE NOT ALONE ............................................................ 1
HEADWATERS FOREST REDWOOD'S LAST
    STAND (FINAL LEASE) ................................................ 3
IN GANDERS' FIELD ............................................................ 7
BORIS AND THE TRICKSTER ............................................. 9
A SOUTHERN SHIP OFF COURSE ................................... 10
THE HATCHBACK OF BY ..........U ................................... 11
CARE ..................................................................................... 12
BALANCE AT LAST........OR ELSE ................................... 13
-THE-OLDE-GANG-RICH- ................................................ 14
CEASE .................................................................................. 15
THE TORPEDOES OF PROGRESS ................................... 16
NOW ..................................................................................... 18
THE "RIGHT" TART ............................................................ 20
CROWN JEWEL .................................................................. 21
THE ORANGE GANG ......................................................... 22
"SPORTSTERS" THE GREEDY GLADIATORS
    OF ROME II ................................................................... 25
HE IS, AS HIS NAME IMPLIES ......................................... 27
"FLUSH POOBAH" .............................................................. 29
A WHITE MAN'S CRY FOR THE RED MAN'S
    SOUL ............................................................................. 30
MAD DOGS AND CIVILIZED MEN ................................. 32
ALPHA-BETA-SKY .............................................................. 34
HEALTH TO ALL ................................................................ 35
"FED" UP 1980 ..................................................................... 36
DEAR BROTHERS AND SISTERS ..................................... 37

QUEST .......................................................................... 38
TRUTH............................................................................ 39
A TEACHER'S HIDEOUT ............................................ 40
CHILD OF THE DOVE...................................................... 41
THE ORIGINAL HIPPY ................................................ 43
DOORS ........................................................................ 45
WE WILL SEE................................................................ 47
THE SONG .................................................................... 48
GET ABOARD .............................................................. 49
LEARN............................................................................ 51
RABIN ............................................................................ 52
NATURAL HIGH............................................................ 53
THE SACRAMENTO'S .................................................... 55
GOOD MORNING ........................................................ 57
VIETNAM DANCE ........................................................ 58
CROWNED...................................................................... 59
DICK'S ARMEY ............................................................ 60
MOBILIZE...................................................................... 61
IT'S NOT TOO LATE .................................................... 62
CANNON FODDER........................................................ 63
FOR FUTURE CHILDREN TO BELIEVE ...................... 64
THE NEW AMERICAN LABOR MOVEMENT ............ 66
PARTNERS .................................................................... 69
THE SOUND OF WATER................................................ 71
VANITY OF MAN .......................................................... 72
LINUS, "THE LION HEART" ........................................ 73
ON .................................................................................. 74
FIRE PILOTS.................................................................. 75
SOULS OF HOPE............................................................ 76
THE TONGASS................................................................ 78
CO-CO-MO AND WHITE HORSE.................................. 80
LIGHT OUR LIGHT ...................................................... 82
MELANCHOLY BAY ...................................................... 83

FAITH ...... 85
LIVE RIGHT NOW ...... 86
RIDE ON ...... 87
YOU ...... 88
WE ...... 89

# Preface

Philosophy, prose, poems and songs are expressed with passionate and romantic as well as political zest. The author covers a wide variety of subjects, dealing with the sheer beauty of our natural world to comical, political jabs at some of the so-called political leaders of our country. The book also reflects a true love of the animals, plants, rivers, people, trees and seas of this great planet we all live upon. There is humor, beauty, love and sarcasm, as well as history within these pages of hope, promise and love.

# YOU'RE NOT ALONE

GATHER…UNTO THE PEOPLE
ONE AND ALL……. ALL FOR ONE
GATHER…UNTO THE PEOPLE
HEAR THE CALL…..ONE AND ALL

YOU'RE NOT ALONE…….OH NO…YOU'RE NOT ALONE

RATHER…WE BE GOOD PEOPLE
STAND UP TALL…THROUGH IT ALL
RATHER…WE BE GOOD PEOPLE
DO NOT STALL…STAND UP TALL

YOU'RE NOT ALONE…….OH NO…YOU'RE NOT ALONE

POWER…UNTO THE PEOPLE
USE IT WISE…….REALIZE
POWER…BE WITH THE PEOPLE
USE IT WELL…….RING THE BELL

YOU'RE NOT ALONE…….OH NO…YOU'RE NOT ALONE

PEACE…COME TO THE PEOPLE
LET IT BE…….REALITY
PEACE…UNTO THE PEOPLE
FOR ALL TO SEE…….HUMANITY

YOU'RE NOT ALONE…….OH NO…YOU'RE NOT ALONE

YOU'RE NOT ALONE…….OH NO…YOU'RE NOT ALONE

YOU'RE NOT ALONE
YOU'RE NOT ALONE

# HEADWATERS FOREST
# REDWOOD'S LAST STAND
# (FINAL LEASE)

WE FELL FROM SKY TO EARTH
A LONG, LONG TIME AGO
WHEN ROME T'WAS GIVEN BIRTH
THE RAINS BEGAN TO SOW

WE FELL FROM GREAT GRANDFATHERS
WHEN JESUS SPREAD HIS WORD
UPON THIS EARTH, OUR MOTHER
WITH NATIVES, WHO HAD HEARD

THE GREEKS HAD PASSED FROM POWER
WHEN WE BEGAN TO SOW
AS LIVING THINGS WILL FLOWER
OUR ARMS BEGAN TO GROW

WE SPREAD OUT VERY SLOWLY
WITH CANOPIES, OH SO HIGH
IN SHADED GROVES SO HOLY
WHERE BOUGHS IN WIND, WOULD FLY

THE FALL OF ROME CAME SOON
AND YET, WE STOOD OUR GROUND
LIFE DEALT A SAVAGE WOUND
BUT WE WERE STILL AROUND

WHEN KUBLAI KHAN, LORDED EAST
AND RODE O'ER MANY PROVINCE
OUR BOUGHS SPREAD OUT, PERFUMING AIR
WITH FRAGRANT FOREST INCENSE

WE GREW SO EVER SLOWLY
AND REACHED OUT FOR THE SKY
AND YET WE FELT SO LOWLY
TO KINSHIP, OH SO HIGH

CRUSADERS RODE FROM BRITAIN
TO SPAIN'S MOROCCAN BAND
WITH STRENGTH, WE GREW QUITE SMITTEN
WITH OUR HEIGHT, O'ER YOUNGER STAND

WHEN DARKNESS T'WAS THE AGE OF MAN
AND SATAN FLEW O'ER PEOPLE
OUR BOUGHS GREW LONG, WITH OPEN HAND
AND WE BECAME A STEEPLE

WHEN FOG ROLLED IN, OUR BOUGHS WOULD
DRINK
THE COOL PACIFIC DEW-DROPS
THE WISDOM OF OUR LORD, YOU'D THINK
FROM FLOOR, TO STATELY TREE-TOPS

AND INLAND HIGH ON MOUNTAINS
WE GREW WITH SUN AND HEAT
GREAT WIDE SEQUOIA FOUNTAINS
WHOSE WIDTHS, WERE MANY FEET

EUROPA THRIVED WITH GREATNESS
GREAT HEIGHT T'WAS GAINED BY WE
WHILE HUMANS WERE STILL FAITHLESS
OUR SUNLIT BOUGHS WOULD SEE

MAGNA-CARTA PAVED THE ROAD
AS WE GREW THICK AND STRONG
DEMOCRACY, RANG OUT AN ODE
OUR BOUGHS AND LEAVES A SONG

WHEN FERDINAND AND ISABELLA
RULED THE SPANISH MANE
COMMISSIONED TO AN OBSESSED FELLA
THOUGHT TO BE INSANE

WE TOWERED O'ER OCEAN BLUE
AND DRANK THE RAINS FROM HEAVEN
AND SIPPED THE SALTY FOGGY DEW
O'ER HUNDRED, TWICE, TIMES SEVEN

AND WHEN AT LAST
THE WHITE MAN CAME
OUR GREATNESS SPREAD
WITH WORLD FAME

AND ONE BY ONE
MY KINSHIP FELL
THE AXE HAD WON
WITH WOOD TO SELL

AND HERE WE ARE, IN MODERN TIMES
OUR KINSHIP LEFT, ARE FEW
THE CLOCK HAS RUNG, ITS MANY CHIMES
MAN'S MERCY SURELY DUE

WE'RE **SEQUOIA GIGANTEA**
AND **SEQUOIA SEMPERVIRONS**
LARGEST EARTHLY KIND OF TREE
OUR SPECIES, FORMING OUR ENVIRONS

HIGH GREAT MOUNTAINS ARE OUR HOST
WHERE SIERRAS MEET NEVADAS
AND ON THE FARTHEST WESTERN COAST
UP ON THE NORTHERN CALIFORNIAS

AND WE ASK FOR **MANKIND'S MERCY**
PLEASE, TO SAVE US FROM DESTRUCTION
LARGEST BEINGS, OH SO EARTHLY
USED FOR MANKIND'S BLIND CONSTRUCTION

FOR OUR NUMBERS ARE, BUT A FEW
AND GREED MUST HERE NOW CEASE
MANKIND'S MERCY'S SURELY DUE
FOR **REDWOODS' FORESTS..............FINAL
LEASE!**

# IN GANDERS' FIELD


T'WAS GANDERS' FIELD
WHERE SOLDIERS RARE
WERE BROUGHT TO YIELD
THEIR LIVES SO FAIR

FOR THESE WERE HEROES
THOUGH USED AS PAWNS
MARKED OFF AS ZEROS
UNBURIED IN LAWNS

BLOWN AWAY
TO "KINGDOM COME"
TO MASK THE EVIL
OF PRESIDENTS "DONE"

REMEMBER IRAN
WHERE HOSTAGES LAY
WHERE ARMS WERE SOLD
THEN SHIPPED FAR AWAY

TO AMERICA CENTRAL
TO START A NEW WAR
FOR "AMERIKA" NORTHERN
TO CLOSE AN OLDE DOOR

THESE SOLDIERS STOOD BRAVE
AND SERVED TO BE RIGHT
EXPLOITED BY LEADERS
WHO'VE BROUGHT ON THEIR NIGHT

T'IS TIME FOR OLD LEADERS
TO NOW, TAKE TO FLIGHT
TO SEE THEIR HORIZON
AND FOREVER SEE NIGHT

T'IS TIME FOR OUR NATION
TO MAKE THINGS RIGHT
FOR THE SOLDIERS OF GANDER
TO FEEL OUR LIGHT

FOR THE SOLDIERS OF FAITH
MUST NOW SEE THEIR WORTH
WITH FREEDOM FOR ALL
AND FOR MANKIND'S REBIRTH

# BORIS AND THE TRICKSTER

T'WAS NO MISTAKE
WHEN RICHARD MET
THE STALINESQUE FIGURE
OF THE FASCISTS REGIME

THEN WITH DISGUST
A BORIS NYET
THE TRICKSTER TO RUSSIA
COULD NOT REDEEM

HIS MANIACAL OBSESSION
FOR POWER AND FORCE
FOR THE FAR RIGHT GOAL
OF WORLD DOMINION

T'WAS BORIS WHO STOOD
TO REJECT HIS COURSE
FOR DEMOCRATIC CHANGE
AND THE FAR RIGHT OPINION

OF GANGSTERS OF HATE
AND "NEW WORLD ORDER"
THREE CHEERS FOR BORIS
AND AGAINST "DICKSORDER"
THREE CHEERS FOR BORIS
"LET DEMOCRACY RING"
THREE CHEERS FOR BORIS
"LET DEMOCRACY SING"

# A SOUTHERN SHIP OFF COURSE


HE'S BEEN AT THE HELM, FAR TOO LONG
IT'S NOW TIME FOR HIM, TO RECEIVE THE
"GONG"
AS HE SPITS, SPURTS AND SPUTTERS
WITH RACIST PIG MUTTERS
THE COURSE WHICH HE PLOTS, IS ALL WRONG


HE DIVIDES THE MASS AS HE CONQUERS
AND HAS ALWAYS BEEN KNOWN TO BE BONKERS
HE'S NOT AT ALL SWELL
AND SOON, HEADED FOR HELL
T'IS ONLY HIS SOUL, WHICH HE CONQUERS


FOR HIS BIGOTRY SHOWS, WITH A SHUDDER
HE SELLS HATRED AND SPITS THROUGH A
STUTTER
IT'S FASCIST SABOTAGE
AND ONLY CAMOUFLAGE
PLEASE! SOMEONE ELSE TAKE HIS SHIPS
RUDDER!

# THE HATCHBACK OF BY..........U


WHO HATCHED HIM OUT
AN ODD PRUDE INDEED
A ZEALOT OF THE OTHER BOOK
FOR OTHERS, HE HAS NO NEED
WHILE FOLLOWING THE ANCIENT CROOK
HIS APPETITE FEEDS HIS GREED
WHILE OTHERS CHOSE NOT TO LOOK
POLYGAMY FORMED THEIR CREED
AND CRAZY ZEALOTS, FROM AMERICA TOOK
WHILE HE WATCHED AMERICA BLEED


A RACIST BY RELIGION
AN ELITIST, BY THE CHOSEN FEW
HE'S DEFINITELY WHITE
AND OF COURSE, ALWAYS "RIGHT"
BUT, I'M SORRY, HIS THOUGHTS ARE ASKEW


HE DOES NOT BELIEVE IN HUMAN CIVIL RIGHTS
NOR THE RIGHT FOR OTHERS TO BELIEVE
IN THEIR FORM OF REVERENCE, TO "REACH
GREAT NEW HEIGHTS"
AND FOR MAN TO BEGIN TO RECEIVE
A MESSAGE TO LOVE AND TO DO IT NOW
AND NOT JUST WITHIN YOUR OWN CREED
FOR NO ONE RELIGION, OF A POWERFUL MAN
HAS THE RIGHT TO INSATIABLE GREED

# CARE

IF THE DECIMATION, MANKIND LEAVES BEHIND
ONLY SHOWS, THAT MAN IS BLIND
TO THE GOOD THINGS IN LIFE
LIKE TREES AND SEAS
WHERE THE BUFFALO ROAMS
AND THERE'S SKY AND AIR
AND IT'S EVERYWHERE
AND A PLANET FOR ALL
AND FOR ALL TO SHARE............WHY DOESN'T
EVERYONE CARE...?

# BALANCE AT LAST........OR ELSE

THERE IS NO REASON WHY
WE CANNOT LIVE ON EARTH
WHILE LIMITING OUR NUMBERS
AND CONTROLLING MAN'S BIRTH
T'IS BETTER THAN WAR
AND KILLING ON THE STREET
SO CONTROLLING OURSELVES
WITH OUR OWN SELF CONTROL
LIFE'S CIRCLE JUST MIGHT BE COMPLETE

# -THE OLDE-GANG-RICH-


HE'S TRYING TO MAKE
"HIS OLDE-GANG-RICH"
AS HE TEARS OUT THE FABRIC
STITCH BY STITCH

THE FABRIC OF AMERICA
OF THE RED WHITE AND BLUE
TO ALL OUR PEOPLE
HE'S BOILED IN A STEW

HIS RIGHT-WING-FASCISTS
HAVE DUG A DITCH
TO BURY THE PEOPLE
FOR THE "OLDE-GANG-RICH"

HE'LL SQUANDER AND LOOT
THE CLASSES BELOW
ESPOUSING FALSE VALUES
HE'S AFTER THE DOUGH

FOR THE "OLDE-GANG-RICH"
AND HIS BABYLON-FACE
DIGS AMERICA'S DITCH
AND IS ONE OF DISGRACE

# CEASE

GRAMM CRACKERS
ALL CRACKED-UP
GOOD OLE BOY
IS READY TO SUP

ON PROGRESS, ON HOPE
ON THE PEOPLE'S DREAMS
THIS MAD-MAN IN OFFICE
WITH HIS FAR-RIGHT EXTREMES

WILL TAKE THIS COUNTRY
OF THE RED, WHITE AND BLACK
AND OF ALL TYPES OF PEOPLE
HE'LL STAB IN THE BACK

HIS WORDS ARE FALSE
AND HAVE ALWAYS BEEN
HIS CLOAK, IS DISGUISE
AND HIS GOAL, A SIN

TO ALL WHO HOPE
FOR LOVE AND PEACE
LET THIS MAN'S VOICE
<u>FINALLY CEASE</u>

# THE TORPEDOES OF PROGRESS


DIVERSIONERY TACTICS
TO GET US OFF THE ISSUES
BY THE FAR, FAR RIGHT
USING THEIR TYPICAL PLOY
OF DIVIDE AND CONQUER TACTICS
OF MISINFORMATION
TO THE SCEPTICAL BUT STILL HOPEFUL NATION

LIES, INNUENDOS, FALSE ACCUSATIONS
ALL TO DIVERT THE AMERICAN PUBLIC
FROM WHAT WE SHOULD REALLY
BE THINKING ABOUT

THAT IS
REBUILDING OUR NATION
WHILE ENCOURAGING DEMOCRACY GLOBALLY
GOING FORWARD, TO REALLY GET THE JOB DONE

THE JOB OF SPARKING OUR GREAT NATION
INTO A LIGHT, NEVER SEEN BEFORE.....
ONE OF EQUAL RIGHTS, TO ALL OUR KINDS
TO REBUILD OUR ROADS, SCHOOLS, RAILROADS,
SHIPPING
AND TO FURTHER THE ELECTRONIC HIGHWAY TO
THE FUTURE
AND GIVE HEALTH CARE TO ALL

TO BOLDLY GO FORTH
TO A NEW BROTHERHOOD AND SISTERHOOD OF
ALL MANKIND
AND TO SEE ONCE AND FOR ALL
THAT WE BELONG TO EARTH
AND WE MUST NOT TREAT IT WITH DISRESPECT
BUT INSTEAD, LOVE IT, OURSELVES
AND ALL THE WILD CREATURES
WHO INHABIT
OUR MOTHER EARTH

# **NOW**


WHAT IS THIS RACE TO REPLACE MAN WITH
MACHINE
COMPUTER OPERATED
TO END THE EMPLOY OF MANKIND


WHAT IS THIS RACE FROM ONE UNDEVELOPED
NATION
TO ANOTHER, ONLY TO SEEK SLAVE LABOR
WITH NO RULES TO LOVE MOTHER EARTH


WHAT IS THIS ENORMOUS INFLUX OF THIRD
WORLD PEOPLE
TO LOWER THE WAGES OF ALL WHO LIVE AND
WORK
IN EUROPE, THE U.S.A., CANADA AND AUSTRALIA


NO SOCIETY CAN ABSORB THE WORLD'S
POPULATION
NO SOCIETY OR CIVILIZATION CAN LIVE ON A
SERVICES ECONOMY ALONE
THIRD WORLD NATIONS MUST STRIVE FOR
DEMOCRACY AND PROSPERITY


ALL OF MANKIND MUST HELP TO PRODUCE FOR
THE GOOD OF ALL
BUT COMPETITION THROUGH EXPORTS, IS A
NEVER ENDING RACE
WHICH NO ONE WILL WIN

EACH NATION MUST PRODUCE FOR THE
COMMON GOOD OF ITS OWN
EACH NATION MUST PRODUCE GOODS OF STAPLE
FOR ITS OWN
AND TRADE ONLY GOODS WHICH OTHER
NATIONS CANNOT PRODUCE

WE ALL MUST PRODUCE WITH PRIDE
AND TRADE WITH ONE ANOTHER ON EVEN KEELS
WE MUST MODERNIZE WITH TOTAL REGARD TO
NATURE
AND COMPASSION FOR ALL LIVING
BEINGS…………..NOW

# THE "RIGHT" TART

A MARY MAGDALEN SHE'S NOT
A RIGHT-WING TART
FOR THE RIGHT-WING SOT
LIKE A FISH ON A HOOK
THIS TUNA IS CAUGHT
TO THE RIGHT-WING RICH
THIS SNITCH IS BOUGHT
FOR A MARY MAGDALEN SHE'S NOT

# CROWN JEWEL

CROWN JEWEL, O' THE PACIFIC NORTHWEST
YE MIGHTY PEAKS AND VALLEYS GREEN
YOUR UNTAMED RIVERS, TRULY BLESSED
WITH PASSIONATE ROMANCE AND POWER SEEN
FROM ACTS OF DECIMATION, TO A BALANCED
DREAM

O' LONG SAND JETTIES, FACING WAVES
CARVED BY RIVERS, WILD AND TRUE
SMOOTH PLACID WATERS, PROTECTED BAYS
MASSIVE STORMS, THEN SKIES OF BLUE
GREENING GREAT FORESTS, GLISTENING HUE

PRECIPITOUS MOUNTAINS, RISING FROM BLUE
PAN-PACIFIC SHELF, SKIRTING THE OCEAN
CRASHING THROUGH FOG, RELEASING ITS DEW
GREEN HUMID FOREST, INTOXICATING POTION
A WONDERLAND SCENE, A FANTASY NOTION

PREHISTORIC FOREST, TALL MIGHTY TREES
TALLEST ON EARTH, YOU MIGHTILY SWAY
CRASHING WHITE WAVES, UPON MIGHTY SEAS
ALL CALM TO QUIET, IN A FOGGY GREY
ALL CALM TO QUIET, ON HUMBOLDT BAY

# THE ORANGE GANG


WHEN THE DUKE OF GEORGE
RULED THIS STATE
T'WAS THE COMMON FOLK
WHO LOST THEIR FATE

UPON HIS EXIT
HE TOLD US ALL
OUR ASSETS WERE GREAT
THOUGH TRUTHFULLY SMALL

DAY BY DAY
WE WERE IN THE BLACK
AS THE RED INK FLOWED
THE CARDS WERE STACKED

THEN THE SOUTHERN CITY
GAVE ITS SON
FROM THE OVERBUILT CITY
WHICH NEVER WON

OVER SOUTH SLAVE LABOR
TO BREAK OUR BACKS
WHILE HE WATCHED OUR STATE'S
OPENING CRACKS

THESE ARE THE LOT
OF THE OLDE ORANGE GANG
WHO SOLD OUT OUR STATE
WITH A GREAT BIG BANG

LITTLE PEANUTS
TO RONNIE AND DICK
AS THEY ROBBED OUR STATE
THEIR GAME WAS SLICK

BUT WE THE PEOPLE
MUST TAKE IT BACK
TO TEACH OUR KIDS
TO GET ON TRACK

WHICH LEADS OUR STATE
FROM THE DEEP, DEEP HOLE
FOR ALL OUR PEOPLES
TO "SHINE OUR SOULS"

OUR STATE IS GREAT
SO LET'S TAKE IT BACK
TO CHANGE THE RED INK
AND EXCHANGE IT FOR BLACK

OUR PEOPLE ARE GOOD
AND WE ALL KNOW THE WAY
TO CHANGE FROM THE DARKNESS
AND BRING ON THE DAY

LET'S ALL GET TOGETHER
TO STAND AND TO FIGHT
THE ORANGE GANG LEADERS
OF THE FAR OUT RIGHT

LET'S BRING NEW LEADERS
TO THE GOLDEN STATE
TO BRIGHTLY SHINE
**OUR GOLDEN GATE!**

# "SPORTSTERS"
# THE GREEDY GLADIATORS
# OF ROME II

THE "BIG BOYS", ARE MAKING BILLIONS A YEAR
WHILE THE WORKING CLASS SLOBS, CHEER AND
CHEER
AS OUR PRICE FOR GOODS, GOES HIGHER AND
HIGHER
WE FEED THE MACHINE OF "MAD AV'S DESIRE"

FOR THE "GLADIATORS OF ROME II", ARE THE
REASON WE PAY
THE BILLIONS THEY MAKE, ALL COMES FROM
THE LAY
AND THAT'S YOU AND ME BROTHERS AND YOU
AND I SISTERS
THE DOLLARS THEY MAKE, ARE FROM OUR TOIL
AND BLISTERS

I SAY TO YOU NOW, THE PRICE THEY REQUIRE
HITS OUR POCKET BOOKS AND ALWAYS GOES
HIGHER
HOW MUCH FROM THE WORKERS, DO THESE
"GLADS" NEED
AS THEY TAKE FROM OUR POCKETS, WITH
INSATIABLE GREED

I SAY TO YOU NOW, THERE IS A GREAT NEED
TO PUT "SPORT" BACK IN SPORTS AND TO STOP
THE GREED
WE SPONSOR THESE "HEROS, WITH THE PRICES
WE PAY
THERE'S <u>BILLIONS</u> IN SPORTS AND IT COMES
FROM US LAY

# HE IS, AS HIS NAME IMPLIES

LIKE A LEACH
HE SUCKS
THE BLOOD OF HOPE
FROM THE PEOPLE,
WITH AN AGENDA
FOR HE AND THE CHOSEN FEW

AMERICA! AMERICA
WHEN WILL WE LEARN
OF THE DECEPTION
OF THE FEW FAR OUT RIGHT RADICALS

HE KNOWS HIS JOB
HIS JOB IS TO DESTROY
OUR HOPE
AND TO DIVERT US
FROM THE REAL TRUTH

THE TRUTH OF THE
RICH-RIGHT-WING
AND THEIR CONTROL
OVER US ALL

TO BRING US DOWN
AND THUS
RAISE THEIR STATURE
AND WEALTH

LIKE A LEACH
HE PREACHES
AGAINST HOPE
AND AGAINST AMERICA AND
"THE TRUE HOPE"
OF THE AMERICAN PEOPLE
<u>"THE AMERICAN DREAM"</u>

# "FLUSH POOBAH"

OH CORPULENT ONE
GRAND WIZARD OF HATE
"FLUSH POOBAH"
YOUR MASS
OUTWEIGHS
YOUR EFFLUENT OF HATRED
AND DECEITFUL
MONEY-MAKING
SCHEME…………..
ACHTUNG FLUSH
ACHTUNG FLUSH
YOUR I.Q. IS TWO
AND YOU KNOW WHO
WILL JUDGE YOU
IN
THE END

# A WHITE MAN'S CRY
# FOR THE RED MAN'S SOUL

NATIVES OF AMERICA
STAND UP TALL
BE TRUE, BE BRAVE
AND DO NOT STALL

NATIVES OF AMERICA
BE TRUE AND BE BRAVE
FOR THIS LAND OF AMERICA
IS YOURS NOW TO SAVE

FOR YOU KNOW THE WAY
AND YOU ALWAYS HAVE
YOUR SPIRITUAL BEING
IS THE HEALING SALVE

YOUR WAYS HAVE FALTERED
THROUGH NO FAULT OF YOURS
WHILE YOU'VE WATCHED OUR MOTHER
STAVE OFF ITS SORES

BE TRUE TO YOUR FATHERS
BE TRUE TO OUR EARTH
BE TRUE TO YOUR MOTHERS
TO GIVE A REBIRTH

A REBIRTH OF VALUES
TO LOVE AND TO CARE
FOR MOTHER EARTH'S MANTLE
CAN NO LONGER BARE

THE BRUTAL ATTACKS
WHICH SHE HAS ENDURED
FROM THE RACE OF DESTRUCTION
SHE MUST BE INSURED

NATIVES OF AMERICA
AND LOVERS OF EARTH
GIVE THE GREAT MANTLE
A CHANCE FOR REBIRTH

# MAD DOGS
# AND CIVILIZED MEN


WHEN IN 1994
NEARING THE YEAR 2000
MANKIND, CAN STAND BY
AND WATCH
A MODERN CIVILIZATION FALL
TO ITS' KNEES…………..
WATCH A FASCIST POWER
DESTROY ALL THAT IS
CIVILIZATION…………..
TEARING THE VERY FABRIC
OF MANKIND
THE BODIES AND HEARTS AND SOULS
OF MANKIND
THE BRUTAL SAVAGERY OF A FEW
WHO ARE STARK RAVING MAD………
THEN, THAT TIME HAS COME TO
PUT THE MAD DOGS
ASLEEP……………………..

EUROPA, EUROPA, U.S.A.
WHEN WILL YOU EVER LEARN
WILL YOU EVER LEARN………
WITH ITALY NEXT
UPON YOUR DOORSTEP
WHEN WILL YOU EVER LEARN
TO PUT THE MAD DOGS ASLEEP NOW
AND SAVE
CIVILIZATION FOR TODAY AND TOMORROW
TO SAVE THE BROTHERS AND SISTERS
OF CIVILIZATION TODAY
WILL SAVE YOU AND I, TOMORROW
AND FOR TOMORROWS, TOMORROWS

# ALPHA-BETA-SKY

AZURE
BLUE
CLOUDS
DEW
EFFORTLESSLY
FLOATING
GLORIOUS
HUE
INTENSE
JOY
KNOWINGLY
LOVING
MOVEMENT
NEVER-ENDING
OMINOUSLY
POWERFUL
QUENCHING
RAINS
SENSUALLY
TENDER
UNDULATING
VORTEX
WARMING
XENON
YIELDING
ZENITH

# HEALTH TO ALL

HOW CAN ANYONE
NOT WANT
HEALTH CARE FOR ALL
ONCE AND FOR ALL

CAN ANYONE, RICH OR POOR
INSULATE THEMSELVES
FROM GERMS, DISEASE
AND PESTILENCE

DO WE WANT
THE DEGRADATION
AND FILTH
WHICH WILL DESTROY OUR CIVILIZATION

FROM WHICH NO WEALTH
CAN POSSIBLY REMOVE ITSELF
AND THUS NOT BECOME
ILL AND DISEASED ITSELF

I THINK NOT
I KNOW NOT
HEALTH TO ALL
WILL SAVE US ALL

NOW!

# "FED" UP 1980

6%
7%
8%
NINE?

10%
11%
12%
"FINE"?

13&14
"THE FED'S OUT TO DINE"
15 AND SO ON
"IT OUGHT TO BE A CRIME"

# DEAR BROTHERS AND SISTERS

CARRY ON…DON'T TARRY ON
BUT CARRY ON…SISTERS AND BROTHERS

SAIL ON…RAIL ON
HALE ON…SWEET SISTERS AND BROTHERS

DON'T BAIL-OUT…DON'T SELL-OUT
DO NOT DOUBT…DEAR BROTHERS AND SISTERS

RALLY-ON…WOE-BE-GONE
JUST CARRY-ON…OH BROTHERS AND SISTERS
SWEET SISTERS AND BROTHERS

PLEASE CARRY–ON…DON'T BE GONE
COME ALONG…ALL BROTHERS AND SISTERS
SWEET SISTERS AND…BROTHERS

# QUEST

HITHER COME
YE FELLOW BEINGS
TO QUEST OUR GOAL
OF LEARNED MINDS
COMPASSION SHOWN
TO SOOTHE OUR WOUNDS
AND GROW TO SHOW
OUR SOULS OF FAITH
AND TRAVEL NOT
OUR DEAD END ROADS

WE SEARCH FOR LOVE
AS ALL HAVE DONE
TO EASE OUR ANXIOUS THOUGHTS
AND TEMPER OUR LIVES
AS IF TO GROW
AS ONE
YET STILL STAY THE INDIVIDUALS
WE OF COURSE...ARE

TRAVEL THIS JOURNEY
TOGETHER WE DO
FOR WE MUST...IN ORDER NOT
TO CREATE DISORDER
DESTRUCTION AND DECAY
AND FOR THIS REASON
**WE SHALL ENDURE!**

# TRUTH

TELL THE TRUTH ABOUT J.F.K.
TELL THE TRUTH ABOUT R.F.K.
TELL THE TRUTH ABOUT L.B.J.
TELL THE TRUTH ABOUT MARTIN K.
TELL THE TRUTH ABOUT JAMES EARL RAY
TELL THE TRUTH ABOUT LENNON J.
TELL THE TRUTH ABOUT EDGAR J.
TELL THE TRUTH ABOUT MALCOLM X.
COME ON PEOPLE, TELL ME WHO'S NEXT
TELL THE TRUTH, ABOUT VIET-NAM
AND WHAT'S THE TRUTH ABOUT UNCLE SAM
WHERE IS TWENTY-FIRST CENTURY MAN
I'M COLOR BLIND
AND I DON'T MIND
THE COLOR, THAT YOU ARE
I'M COLOR BLIND
AND I DON'T MIND
THE COLOR, THAT YOU ARE
THE COLOR THAT YOU ARE
THE COLOR THAT YOU ARE

# A TEACHER'S HIDEOUT


ON AN ISLAND, ON A SOUND
WHERE THE FORESTS ARE RENOWNED
WHERE THE EAGLES' FLIGHTS ARE FREE
AND ITS ISLANDS MEET THE SEA

DWELLS A TEACHER AT HIS TRADE
IN A CABIN, HE HAS MADE
SURROUNDED BY A SEA
WHERE THE FISHES, COME TO BE

IN THE FORESTS, THICK AND SOFT
PERCH THE NESTS OF BIRDS ALOFT
WHERE THE WHALES COME TO FEASTS
AND THE BEARS, ARE KINGS OF BEASTS

WHERE THE FISHES LAY THEIR ROE
AND THE BUCK, SEEKS OUT THE DOE
SPANISH MOSSES, ALL GROW GREEN
HANG A FLORAL FOREST SCENE

ON A SPLENDOR COVE OF BLUE
WITH A SOFT AND FUZZY DEW
DWELLS THIS TEACHER, OF THE YOUNG
WHERE NATURE'S REGAL SONG IS SUNG

# CHILD OF THE DOVE

JOHN LENNON, WAS A PROPHET
AND ALL HE SAID WAS LOVE
AN INTRICATE BY NATURE
A CHILD OF THE DOVE

AND ALL HE SAID WAS LOVE YOURSELF
AND ALL OF THOSE AROUND
AND TO ALL LIFE, BE TRIED AND TRUE
AND SEE OUR SOULS BE CROWNED

THAT'S WHY…..JOHN LENNON IS IN HEAVEN
AND NIXON IS IN HELL
"TRICKY-DICK SWORE, HE'D GET THAT BOY"
BUT LENNON SAID NO SELL

HE'S RISEN FOR THE LOVE HE GAVE
TO ALL THE WORLD AROUND
AND SHOWN US, HOW TO LOVE
…..THAT'S WHY HE'S HEAVEN BOUND

A SENSITIVE…MAN OF SOUL
A HEART SO TRIED AND TRUE
A LOVER OF EDEN EARTH
AND AROUND OUR SKY OF BLUE

AND HE SANG HIS SONGS OF LOVE AND TRUTH
AND HIS MUSIC ROUND THE WORLD
AND STOOD AGAINST THE MIGHTY FEW
FOR EVERY BOY AND GIRL

THAT'S WHY….JOHN LENNON IS IN HEAVEN
AND NIXON IS IN HELL
TRICKY-DICK SWORE, HE'D GET THAT BOY
BUT LENNON SAID NO SELL

HE'S RISEN FOR THE LOVE HE GAVE
TO ALL THE WORLD AROUND
AND SHOWN US, HOW TO LOVE
THAT'S WHY….HE'S HEAVEN BOUND

# THE ORIGINAL HIPPY


JESUS WAS A HIPPY
AND HE'LL ALWAYS LIVE IN ME
EVERYWHERE I LOOK AROUND
I KNOW THAT I CAN SEE
THE BEAUTY WHICH SURROUNDS US ALL
WILL LET OUR SOULS BE FREE
FOR JESUS WAS A HIPPY
AND HE'LL ALWAYS BE WITH ME

HIS CHURCH IS UNDERNEATH A TREE
OR WAY OUT ON THE SEA
ON THE PLAINS, O'ER FERTILE GRASS
THE BEAUTY'S THERE TO SEE
HE'S FULL OF LOVE AND ALL HE ASKS
IS WHY CAN'T WE JUST BE
FOR JESUS WAS A HIPPY
AND HE GIVES HIS LOVE FOR FREE

HIS SHADES OF COLOR O'ER THE WORLD
ARE PEOPLE HE SET FREE
AND ROUND THE WORLD, OUR DIFFERENCES
ARE CLEARLY THERE TO SEE
BUT HE'S AROUND AND ALL HE ASKS
IS WHY CAN'T WE JUST BE
FOR JESUS WAS A HIPPY
AND HE GIVES HIS LOVE FOR FREE

HIS WORD IS PEACE FOR EVERYONE
AROUND THIS WORLD OF OURS
TO TELL MANKIND A SIMPLE TRUTH
DON'T WASTE AWAY THE HOURS
BUT BLOSSOM AS IN SPRINGTIME
AND SHOW THE WORLD YOUR FLOWERS
FOR JESUS WAS A HIPPY
AND HE GIVES HIS LOVE FOR FREE

# DOORS

PEACE IS BREAKING OUT ALL OVER
WHILE FASCISTS STRIVE TO MAKE THEIR WARS
ONE WITH LOVE
AND ONE WITH HATE
AND ONLY ONE, WILL OPEN UP THE DOORS

DOORS OF LIGHT AND DOORS OF PEACE
TO FORWARD THINKING, SOULS OF HOPE
SOULS WHO YEARN
FOR TRANQUIL PEACE
THERE IS BUT ONE, TO STAND AND COPE

WITH ACTS OF PEACE, IN HIS HEART
HE TRAVELS ROUND THE WORLD
TO GIVE A SMILE
AND THEN A HUG
TO SHOW THE SOULS UNFURLED

TO BRING TOGETHER ENEMIES
WHO'VE WARRED FOR MANY YEARS
TO NO AVAIL
TO EITHER SIDE
AS HE WIPES AWAY THEIR TEARS

THIS IS AMERICA'S PRESIDENT
WITH A TEAM, WHICH CAN'T BE MATCHED
THEY WORK FOR PEACE
FOR EVERY SIDE
TO OPEN DOORS LONGED LATCHED
THE DOORS OF OLD JERUSALEM
THE DOORS OF PALESTINE
THE DOORS OF DUBLIN
BELFAST TOO
TO MAKE OUR WORLD SHINE

TO BRING A PEACE
TO HAITI
TO SHOW DEMOCRACY
TO SYRIA AND LEBANON
TO SET ALL PEOPLES FREE

TO BRING THE BRITISH, PEACE OF MIND
TO SAVE THE BALKANS TOO
TO STOP THE WARRING
OF MANKIND
TO BUILD A PEACE THAT'S TRUE

YES, THIS IS AMERICA'S PRESIDENT
IN NINETEEN-NINETY-FIVE
A MAN OF PEACE
AND STRENGTH FOR ALL
TO KEEP OUR LOVE ALIVE

# WE WILL SEE


AS THE PEACE-NIKS
COME TO POWER
DON'T CHANGE THEIR FINAL HOUR
DESTINY CANNOT BE ALTERED
NOR CHANGED IN ANY WAY
FOR THE WORLD HAS WAITED PATIENTLY
FOR "PEACE, TO CLAIM ITS DIGNITY"
AND THE "PEOPLES" RIGHT TO LOVE
WILL SEE ITS "GOLDEN DAY"

# THE SONG

THE "RIGHT"
ARE WRONG
THEY CANNOT "SING THE SONG"
THE SONG OF PEACE
AND HARMONY
THE "SONG OF LOVE"
AND UNITY
THE "SONG OF HOPE"
TRANQUILITY
THE SONG ELUDES THEIR SOULS

# GET ABOARD

PEOPLE COME TOGETHER NOW
TO CHANGE THIS WORLD OF OURS
FOR THE CLOCK HAS RUNG ITS MANY CHIMES
TO WASTE AWAY THE HOURS

IT MATTERS NOT, WHAT RACE YOU ARE
FOR NOW THE RACE IS ON
TO GET TOGETHER AS A FORCE
BEFORE THE CHANCE HAS GONE

FOR THERE'S STILL TIME
DON'T FOOL YOURSELF, AND GIVE UP ALL YOUR
HOPE
FOR IF WE BIND, AS HUMAN KIND
I'M SURE THAT WE CAN COPE

WITH ALL THE PROBLEMS WHICH EXIST
WE'LL ACT AS ONE WITH STRENGTH
AND COME TOGETHER, ALL AS ONE
WITH DEEDS OF LASTING LENGTH

TO CONQUER HATE AND BUILD OUR WORLD
WITH PEACE AND LOVE FOR ALL
TO ACT AS HUMANS, GOOD AND TRUE
OUR MOVEMENT SHALL NOT FALL

IT'S NOW THE TIME TO GET ABOARD
AND HUG YOUR FELLOW MAN
TO FEEL THE HIGH OF LOVE AGAIN
AND JEALOUS HATRED BAN

TO FEEL THE HIGH AND TRUST OF LOVE
TO GIVE IT ALL YOU'VE GOT
TO FREE THE SYMBOL, OF THE DOVE
WHICH CHRIST HAS ALWAYS TAUGHT

# LEARN

SINCE THE BEGINNING OF TIME
MAN HAS ROAMED THIS EARTH
TO LOOK AND SEARCH
FOR SOME PLACE NEW.............
OR TO RUN AWAY
FROM WHAT WAS THERE
KNOWING THAT
HE COULD NOT ENDURE
MAN'S INHUMANITY TO MAN
OR THAT WHICH HE SAW
AS THE CIVILIZATION OF MAN
AND THE DESTRUCTION OF THE ENVIRONMENT
AROUND HIM
AND HIS NATURAL SURROUNDINGS
WHICH HE HIMSELF SEEMED TO DESTROY
WITHOUT LEARNING THAT HE HIMSELF
DESTROYED EVERYTHING AROUND HIM
INCLUDING HIMSELF
WILL WE NEVER LEARN?

# RABIN

I CRIED THE DAY, YITZAK DIED
WITH MELANCHOLY TEARS, I SIGHED
A WARRIOR FIRST, WHO TURNED TO PEACE
TO SHOW HIS WISH, FOR WAR TO CEASE

A GENTLE MAN, WHO'D SEEN THE WORST
OF DEATH AND PAIN, HE TRULY CURSED
TO BRING UPON A PEACE AT LAST
TO STOP THE HATRED, OF THE PAST

A CHAMPION OF FAITH AND TRUTH
TO CALM HIS PEOPLE AND TO SOOTHE
THE SCARS OF WAR AND TERROR TOO
TO BRING A LOVE AND PEACE LONG DUE

TO ISRAEL AND PALESTINE
TO MAKE THEIR PEOPLES AURA SHINE
TO SHOW THE SYMBOL OF THE DOVE
TO TURN THE HATRED, INTO LOVE

HE GAVE HIS LIFE FOR FREEDOM'S CAUSE
FOR PEACE, FOR LOVE OF NATURE'S LAWS
TO STOP THE KILLING OF MANKIND
FOR JEWS AND ARABS, SOULS TO BIND

RABIN AND PEACE, MUST LONG ENDURE
FOR MIDDLE-EAST, TO HEAL AND CURE
FROM SICKNESS LONG, ENDURED BY MAN
FOR DEATH AND HATRED, SOULS TO BAN

# NATURAL HIGH

IF YOU KNOW THE FEELING
OF A VOID IN YOUR HEART
YOU SHOULD KNOW, YOU'RE DEALING
WITH, THE FINE LINE, OF ART
OF LOVING MAN AND ALL OUR EARTH
OF LOVING YOU, YOURSELF
OF LOVING SISTERS, BROTHERS TOO
WITH LOVE, YOU'LL FIND YOUR WEALTH

IF YOU FEEL, YOU'VE LOST YOUR HEART
AND LIVING, DAY BY DAY
IT'S TIME FOR YOU, TO MAKE A START
AND SHINE A GOLDEN RAY
OF PEACE AND LOVE, FOR ALL MANKIND
IT'S TIME TO SHINE AWAY
IT'S TIME, TO LOVE, YOUR FELLOW BEINGS
AND SHINE, A BRIGHTER DAY

IF YOU FEEL, YOU'VE LOST, YOUR SOUL
AND DON'T KNOW WHERE, TO TURN
JUST OPEN UP, YOUR HEART AND SOUL
YOU'LL OPEN UP, TO LEARN
THROUGH CLEAR-BLUE SKIES, YOUR HEART
WILL FLY
AND YOU WILL REALIZE
THAT LOVE BETWEEN, YOUR FELLOW BEINGS
WILL OPEN UP, YOUR EYES

IF YOU WISH, FOR HARMONY
WITH BEINGS, ON OUR EARTH
AND GIVE IT, WITH SINCERITY
HEARTS WILL GAIN REBIRTH
OF LOVE AND PEACE AND MUSIC TOO
TO HEAR, THE PEOPLES CRY
FOR LOVE, TO GIVE US, PEACE OF MIND
IT'S ALL, A NATURAL HIGH……
WITH LOVE, WE'LL ALL GET BY

# THE SACRAMENTO'S

WAY UP NORTH, WHERE THE MOUNTAINS GROW
FROM THE VALLEY FAR BELOW
SNOW-CAPPED PEAKS, IN THE CLEAR-BLUE SKIES
RELEASE THE WATERS FLOW
SACRAMENTO....WHERE THE WATER FREELY
FLOWS
SACRAMENTO....WHERE THE MOUNTAINS
GATHER SNOW
SACRAMENTO....WHERE THE VALLEY'S FAME IS
KNOWN
SACRAMENTO....OH THE WATER

SHASTA PEAKS, WITH LIGHTNING STREAKS
ALMOST THREE MILES IN THE SKY
LASSEN PEAKS, WITH VOLCANIC LEAKS
ALL A NATURAL HIGH
SACRAMENTO....IS THE VALLEY'S GIVEN NAME
SACRAMENTO....WITH ITS RIVER CALLED THE
SAME
SACRAMENTO....IS THE UPPER VALLEY'S FAME
SACRAMENTO....OH THE MOUNTAINS

YOLLA-BOLLY, IS A MOUNTAIN PEAK
IT'S A VIEW, FOR ALL TO SEEK
ON THE WESTERN SIDE, WHERE THE SUN GOES
TO HIDE
IS WHERE THIS MOUNTAIN PEAKS
SACRAMENTO....WHERE THE MOUNTAINS
GATHER SNOW
SACRAMENTO....WHERE THE VALLEY'S FAME IS
KNOWN
SACRAMENTO....WHERE THE BEAUTY HERE IS
SHOWN
SACRAMENTO....OH THE VALLEY

TRINITY ALPS, ON THE NORTHWEST SIDE
OF THE VALLEY FAR BELOW
SISKIYOUS, ON THE NORTHERN END
GLISTEN GOLDEN GLOW
SACRAMENTO....WHERE THE WATER FREELY
FLOWS
SACRAMENTO....WHERE THE MOUNTAINS
GATHER SNOW
SACRAMENTO....WHERE THE VALLEY'S FAME IS
KNOWN
SACRAMENTO....OH THE BEAUTY

# GOOD MORNING

THE MOON IS FULL AND BRIGHT
ON AN INDIAN SUMMER NIGHT
YET IT'S WINTER, IN THE MOUNTAINS
IN THE MID-NOVEMBER DAYS

AS THE CLOUDS APPEAR BY MORNING
THEY GIVE THE SAILORS' WARNING
AS THE EARTH TURNS TOWARDS THE SUN
IT SHINES ITS GOLDEN RAYS

OMINOUS CLOUDS, DARK AND BLACK
FLOW ABOVE HORIZONS CRACK
WITH EDGES OF BRIGHT-GOLDEN LIGHT
MY EYES, THEY CLEARLY GAZE

AND AGAIN, BY EARLY MORNING
THEY'VE LOST THEIR SAILORS' WARNING
AS THE CLOUDS, FLOW BY THE SUN
IT SHINES ITS GOLDEN GLAZE

# **VIETNAM DANCE**

DANCE ON THE GRAVES
OF THE VIETNAM DEAD
DANCE FOR THEIR SOULS
TO END THEIR DREAD

GIVE THEM LIGHT
TO WARM THEIR SOULS
GIVE THEM SIGHT
TO REACH THEIR GOALS

TO END THEIR LOSS
AND GIVE THEM WORTH
AND WELCOME THEM BACK
TO OUR MOTHER EARTH

# CROWNED

LAYING ON A GRASSY KNOLL
O'ER LOOKING MOUNTAINS SPLENDOR
UNDERNEATH THE OAKS AND PINES
LIFE'S SUBTLENESS IS TENDER

GAZING OFF INTO A SKY
A BREEZE WITH COOLNESS BLOWS
ACROSS THE HILLTOPS, TREETOPS LOOM
WITH A PEAK, WHERE IT STILL SNOWS

IT IS NOW EARLY AUGUST
YET GREENERY ABOUNDS
WITH SKIES OF BLUE AND A GLORIOUS HUE
THERE'S A FREEDOM WHICH SURROUNDS

SURROUNDS THE SOUL WITH HARMONY
AND GIVES THE HUMAN STRENGTH
AND FILLS THE HEART SO FAITHFULLY
WITH LASTING DEEDS OF LENGTH

FOR THIS IS THE DANCE OF HARMONY
OUR NATURAL WORLD AROUND
IT'S ALL OUR WORLD, AND FOR ALL LIFE
OUR EARTH'S BEEN TRULY CROWNED

*Quentin M. Codding*

# DICK'S ARMEY

YOU! SHUT IT DOWN
AND WITHOUT COMMON GROUND
AS OUR GOVERNMENT, CAME TO A HALT

YET EVERY EVIL FROWN
WILL NEVER BRING US DOWN
FOR WE KNOW IT'S THE RIGHT-WING'S FAULT

FOR YOU CARE NOT FOR
THE COMMON PERSON'S CHORE
ON "THE DREAM" YOU HAVE MADE YOUR
ASSAULT!

FOR THE PEOPLE'S RIGHT
TO STAND UP AND FIGHT
WILL PROVE, "THAT WE ARE THE SALT"!

# **MOBILIZE**

WE IN THE U.S.A.
MUST MOBILIZE TO ACTION
AND FORM A NEW MOVEMENT
TO EMPLOY AMERICANS IN AMERICA
AT HIGHER LEVELS OF MONETARY GAIN AND
REWARD
AND TO INSURE A STRONG BUT SCEPTICAL
POPULATION
THAT WE CAN MOBILIZE QUICKLY
TO PUT A VAST SEA OF AMERICAN SOULS
BACK TO WORK
WHILE BETTERING THE U.S.A.
ECONOMICALLY, ENVIRONMENTALLY,
PSYCHOLOGICALLY & PHYSICALLY

FOR WITHOUT A LARGE AND STRONG MIDDLE
CLASS
THE ENTIRE SYSTEM OF FREE ENTERPRISE
AND DEMOCRACY IS DOOMED TO FAIL
AND NOTHING IS BOUGHT
THEREFORE NOTHING IS PRODUCED
AND NOTHING IS GAINED

*Quentin M. Codding*

# IT'S NOT TOO LATE


WHY DOES MAN WAR?
WHY DO WE COMPETE?
WHY DON'T WE CO-OPERATE
WHY MUST WE HATE?


WHO IS MAN?
WHO CAN WE DENY LOVE TO?
WHO MUST SAVE US FROM OURSELVES?
WHO DO WE REALLY HATE?


HOW LONG WILL WE SURVIVE?
HOW MUST WE LIVE?
HOW DO WE FIND LOVE?
HOW IS IT, THAT WE HATE?


WHERE MIGHT WE FIND OURSELVES?
WHERE DOES LOVE COME FROM?
WHERE DO WE WANT TO GO?
WHERE ARE OUR HEARTS?


WHEN WILL WE FIND LOVE?
WHEN WILL WE HAVE PEACE?
WHEN WILL WE CO-OPERATE?
WHEN WILL WE CEASE TO HATE?

# CANNON FODDER

HYPOCRITICAL MOUTHPIECE
FOR CROSSING THE FIRE
MAKING SOMETHING
FROM NOTHING
WHILE HE RAISES OUR IRE

LINED UP STRAIGHT
WITH THE FAR OUT RIGHT
CONFUSING THE MASSES
FOR THE RIGHT-WING ASSES
HIS WORDS, ONLY BRING ON A BLIGHT

# FOR FUTURE CHILDREN TO BELIEVE

ALONG THE UPPER, SACRAMENTO
A PULP MILL FLOWS INTO ITS WATERS
DIOXIN TOXIC WASTES ARE FLOWING
TO TURN ITS COLD CLEAN WATER HOTTER
AND KILL THE CUTTHROAT AND THE SALMON
AND TAINT THE BEAUTY OF ITS FLOW
TO KILL THE MOUNTAIN WATER
TO KILL THE RIVER TOO
TO KILL THE FRESH STREAM WATER
TO TURN IT BROWN, FROM BLUE

ALONG THE UPPER, SACRAMENTO
THEY RAPE THE FORESTS FOR THE DOUGH
TO GRIND THE TREES, INTO A POWDER
AND CHANGE THE RIVERS NATURAL FLOW
AND STRIP THE LAND, OF ALL ITS COVER
AND RAPE THIS EARTH, OUR MOTHER
TO KILL THE FORESTS GREEN
TO KILL THE RIVER TOO
TO MAKE THEIR DOLLARS GREEN
AND DIRTY WATERS, CLEAR AND BLUE

ALONG THE UPPER SACRAMENTO
THE MIGHTY PULP MILL, FLAUNTS ITS POWER
WITH CHIP TRUCKS, ROARING DOWN THE ROAD
ALONG THE BANKS, THE SMOKE-STACKS TOWER
AND TOXIC WASTE IS DUMPED ALL OVER
THE TANKER TRUCKS, THEY DUMP THEIR LOADS
TO KILL THE DRINKING WATER
TO KILL THE FOWL THAT FLY
TO KILL OUR SONS AND DAUGHTERS
SHOULDN'T PEOPLE, WONDER WHY?

WE WANT TO FREE, THE SACRAMENTO
AND CLEAR, THE AIR WE BREATHE
TO SAVE THE WILD WONDERS
FOR FUTURE CHILDREN, TO BELIEVE
FOR FUTURE CHILDREN, TO BELIEVE

# THE NEW AMERICAN LABOR MOVEMENT

WE LABOR AND TOIL AND STRIVE TO BE
LOYAL AND TRUE, TO THE "COMPANY"
AFTER SERVING FOR YEARS, THEY THEN LAY US
OFF
AS OWNERS AND CEO'S, FLAGRANTLY SCOFF

AT THE VALUE OF WORKERS AND OUR LOYALTY
AS THEY ELEVATE THEMSELVES, TO HIGH
ROYALTY
DISPOSING OF WORKERS, AS THOUGH WE WERE
PAWNS
SHACKLING THE WORKERS, WITH INVISIBLE
BONDS

OF LOWER PAY AND MENIAL JOBS
THE RICH BECOME RICHER, FROM THE WORKERS,
THEY ROB
ROB US OF PAY AND OUR DIGNITY
BREAK US, THEY SAY, OF OUR UNITY

NO UNIONS, NO HONOR AND LOWER THEIR PAY!
AS THE RICH BECOME RICHER, BY THE WORK OF
THE LAY
THE FAT CATS, GROW FATTER, AS WE ALL FALL
DOWN
AS THE RICH, BECOME RICHER, THEY PUT ON
THEIR CROWN

TO DOMINATE WORKERS AND TAKE AWAY
RIGHTS
THE RICH, FAT CATS, REACH FOR NEW HEIGHTS
THEIR GREED, BEYOND REASON, WITH NO END IN
SIGHT
AS THEY BREAK DOWN THE WORKERS AND
BRING ON A BLIGHT

OF LOWER EXPECTATIONS AND INSECURITY
TO TAKE AWAY RIGHTS, IN "THE LAND OF THE
FREE"
IT'S TIME FOR THE WORKERS, TO STAND AND TO
FIGHT
TO STAND UP TALL AND TURN WRONG INTO
RIGHT

TO UNIONIZE WORKERS, FOR THE GOOD OF ALL
TO GROW A NEW MOVEMENT, WHICH SHALL NOT
FALL
TO BRING ABOUT CHANGE AND RIGHT THE
WRONG
TOGETHER, THE PEOPLE, SHALL STAND UP
STRONG

FOR IF "WE THE PEOPLE", FIGHT FOR WHAT'S
RIGHT
THE PEOPLE AS ONE, "SHALL THEN SEE THE
LIGHT"
THE LIGHT OF FREEDOM, THE LIGHT OF
STRENGTH
FOR DECENT PAY AND JOBS OF LENGTH

FOR "WE THE PEOPLE", DESERVE BETTER PAY
TO GAIN BACK OUR RIGHTS AND TO SEE A NEW
DAY
A DAY OF BRIGHTNESS, A DAY OF NEW SIGHT
A NEW DAY OF VISION AND A NEW DAY OF LIGHT

# PARTNERS

ABOVE FALL RIVER VALLEY
ON A BENCH THAT'S KNOWN AS DAY
THERE LIVE TWO SPIRITS FULL OF LOVE
WHO PASS THE TIME AWAY

THEIR HEARTS ARE STRONG AND TRUE
THEY GIVE TO HUMAN-KIND
EACH DAY THEY PRAY, FOR PEACE AND LOVE
THEIR QUEST IS PEACE OF MIND

THEY'VE WORKED TO MAKE THEIR HOUSE A
HOME
WITH REVERENCE TO THE LAND
THEY BUILT THEIR HOME WITH LOVING CARE
TO MAKE THEIR HOMESTEAD GRAND

NARY A TREE, HAS BEEN CUT DOWN
THEY BUILT AROUND THEIR GROVES
A RUSTIC WESTERN COWBOY HOUSE
WITH HEAT FROM WOOD FUELED STOVES

THEIR BRIC-A-BRAC AND NICKNAKS TOO
ALL GIVE THEIR HOME A WARMTH
THROUGH SUNNY DAYS AND HOT SUN-RAYS
AND MASSIVE LIGHTNING STORMS

THEY RIDE ON HORSES, STRONG AND TRUE
O'ER MOUNTAINS, WILD AND CLEAN
AND THROUGH THE VALLEY, FAR BELOW
WITH MEADOWS, LUSH AND GREEN

THEIR LOVE HAS GROWN, THROUGH THICK AND
THIN
AND WEATHERED THROUGH THE STORMS
AND EACH AND EVERY DAY THEIR LOVE
HAS TAKEN MANY FORMS

THEY'VE LEARNED TO SEE THE JOY OF LIFE
AND HELD EACH OTHER TIGHT
TO GIVE AND TAKE AND SHOW THEIR LOVE
TO BRING UPON A LIGHT

A LIGHT WHICH COMES TO VERY FEW
ENDURING, STRONG AND TRUE
FOR THOSE WHO WORK TO LOVE THEIR LOVE
THEIR LOVE, COMES SHINING THROUGH

# THE SOUND OF WATER

I'LL NEVER TIRE, OF THE SOUND OF WATER OVER
ROCKS
AND THE SPLASH THAT HYPNOTIZES THE MIND
AND SOUL

AS YOU LOSE THE STRESS, OF MODERN LIVING
ONE FEELS AT PEACE, WITH ALL THAT IS
AROUND YOU

IT IS THE GIFT OF SERENITY, GIVEN TO ALL
WHO MAKE THE TIME TO STOP
AND LISTEN TO "THE SOUND OF WATER"

# VANITY OF MAN


STOP!…. IF YOU CAN
THE VANITY OF MAN
TO DESTROY THAT WHICH "IS"
IS TO DESTROY ALL
THAT IS AROUND
THIS NATURAL WORLD
WHOSE BEAUTY ABOUNDS
AND CANNOT BE IMPROVED UPON
NOR CONQUERED BY MAN
BUT INSTEAD, LIVED AND LOVED UPON……………
AND FOR MAN TO SEE "HIS DAWN"

# LINUS, "THE LION HEART"

LINUS, WAS A PASSIONATE MAN
WHO STOOD UP FOR A CAUSE
A SMALL AND FRAIL, MAN HE WAS
WHO STOOD, TO CHANGE THE LAWS

LINUS STOOD, AGAINST A WAR
A WAR WITHOUT A CAUSE
HE'D DEMONSTRATE, FOR PEACE AND LOVE
TO SHOW WARS MANY FLAWS

LINUS, WON THE NOBEL PRIZE
FOR CHEMISTRY AND FOR PEACE
FOR FUTURE CHILDREN'S PEACE OF MIND
FOR WAR AND DEATH TO CEASE

LINUS WAS A WONDROUS SOUL
A GENIUS AND A FRIEND
TO ALL OF US, WHO'D DEMONSTRATE
HIS STRENGTH AND SOUL, HE'D LEND

LINUS WAS, THE "LION HEART"
TO GUIDE US, TO OUR GOAL
THE GOAL OF PEACE AND LOVE FOR ALL
TO GIVE OUR MOVEMENT "SOUL"

LINUS, WAS A FRIEND TO ALL
WHO YEARNED, FOR WAR TO CEASE
A CHAMPION, FOR ALL MANKIND
"THE LION HEART OF PEACE"

# ON

TURN ON YOUR MIND
AND LIGHT THE WAY
TO A NEW BEGINNING
AND A BRAND NEW DAY

LIGHT UP THE SKY
AND OPEN YOUR MIND
TURN ON YOUR HEAD
AND AWARENESS YOU'LL FIND

GIVE IT YOUR BEST
TO BECOME AWARE
TO CHANGE THIS SYSTEM
SO WE ALL MAY SHARE

THE GOODNESS INSIDE
WHICH WE ALL WANT TO SHOW
TO COME TOGETHER
SO WE ALL MAY KNOW

THE LOVE, WHICH WILL WIN
AND SHOW US THE WAY
TO END THE CORRUPTION
AND BRING ON OUR DAY

TO END THE OLD WORLD
AND BRING ON THE NEW
TO SHINE THROUGH THE CLOUDS
AND LET THE SUN THROUGH

# FIRE PILOTS

FLYING LOW, DOING NINETIES IN THE SKY
WINDS SWEEP THEIR WINGS, AS WE WONDER
WHY
THESE NUTS AND BOLTS, RISK THEIR LIVES
WITH ROARING ENGINES, TURNS, THEN DIVES

FILLED TO THE BRIM, WITH SAVING GRACE
FOR FORESTS LIVES, THESE HEROES CHASE
THE BURNING EMBERS AND ROARING FLARES
WHILE THE PEOPLE LOOK, WITH AMAZING
GLARES

ROARING ENGINES, WINGS ON HIGH
THEY CIRCLE, THEN DROP DOWN, FROM THE SKY
AND SKID UPON, THE TREE TOPS FLY
SWOOPING DOWN, THEN BY AND BY

DROPPING LOADS OF H2O
THESE NUTS AND BOLTS, THEY FLY DOWN LOW
RISKING THEIR LIVES, WITH ADRENALINE'S
FLASH
TO QUENCH THE FOREST'S TREES AND SLASH

THEN CIRCLE ROUND, LIKE SOARING BIRDS
THERE ARE NO THOUGHTS, TO EXPRESS THE
WORDS
OF AMAZEMENT AND THANKS, TO THESE HEROES
ON HIGH
WHO ROAR THEIR ENGINES THROUGH THE SKY

# SOULS OF HOPE

THE MOVEMENT WAS CHASED
BY THE INJUSTICE OF LAW
THE CRUSADE IN HASTE
AND OH HOW THEY SAW

T'WAS TIME FOR FLIGHT
OR FOR PEOPLE TO STAND
TO TURN ON THE LIGHT
AND STRIKE-UP THEIR BAND

THE "RIGHT" CHASED THEM DOWN
AND CORNERED THE LOT
AND EVERY EVIL FROWN
HAD ALL BEEN BOUGHT

THEN ALL AT ONCE
THE CRUSADERS AROSE
PERFORMING GREAT STUNTS
AND WALLOPING BLOWS

AND THE LIGHT SHOWN O'ER
EVERY FACE OF HOPE
AS THE EVIL PURSUERS
HUNG BY THEIR ROPE

AND THERE CAME A SOUL
WHEN WHOM HE TOUCHED
THEY SHINED OF GOLD
AND HOPE THEY CLUTCHED

THEIR SOULS ENTWINED
WITH FEAR NO MORE
THEY BRIGHTLY SHINED
AND OPENED A DOOR

AS HE TOUCHED THEIR SOULS
THEIR RESTLESSNESS CEASED
THEY REALIZED THEIR GOALS
AND HAD FOUND THEIR PEACE

AND IT SPREAD FAR AND WIDE
AND GAVE THEM LIGHT
T'WAS NO REASON TO HIDE
FOR THEY NOW HAD THEIR SIGHT
AND THEIR SIGHT WAS CLEAR
AS THEY SAW CLEAR LIGHT

# THE TONGASS

ON THE AWESOME INLAND PASSAGE
OF THE GREAT STATE OF ALASKA
LIES, THE MIGHTY FOREST TONGASS
LARGEST FOREST OF OUR NATION

ON ITS MANY WONDROUS ISLES
SITKA SPRUCE GROW TALL AND WILD
O'ER THE MIGHTY FOREST TONGASS
ONE CAN ONLY FEEL ELATION

FOR THE CRYSTAL CLEAR-BLUE WATERS
WHICH SURROUND THE FOREST TONGASS
HOST THE CREATURES OF THE OCEAN
SINCE THE TIME OF ALL CREATION

WHALES SWIM ITS COLD CLEAR WATERS
AROUND THE ISLANDS OF THE TONGASS
RICH WITH FISH OF MANY SPECIES
FILL THEIR NICHE IN EVERY STATION

FOR THE LIFE AROUND THE ISLANDS
OF THE FORESTS OF THE TONGASS
LIVE BECAUSE THERE IS A BALANCE
BETWEEN THE FORESTS AND THE WATER

FOR THE FORESTS HOLD THE SOIL
OF THE ISLANDS OF THE TONGASS
RIVERS FEED THE OCEAN'S CREATURES
SALMON, CRAB AND GREAT SEA OTTER

AS THEIR RIVERS FEED THE INLETS
AND THE BAYS OF CLEAR-BLUE SPENDOR
THE GREAT GREEN ISLANDS OF THE TONGASS
MAKE OUR INSIGHT BECOME BROADER

WITH A WISH TO SAVE THESE SPLENDORS
FOR ALL CREATURES OF THE FUTURE
GREAT GREEN EMERALDS ON BLUE SEAS
FOR FISH AND MAMMAL….SON AND DAUGHTER

FOR THERE IS NO OTHER PLACE ON EARTH
WHICH SHOWS ITS PRISTINE BEAUTY
MANKIND'S WISH <u>MUST</u> BE TO SAVE
THE TONGASS FROM MAN'S GREEDY SLAUGHTER

*Quentin M. Codding*

# CO-CO-MO AND WHITE HORSE

WHILE CO-CO-MO AND WHITE HORSE
WERE WANDERING THROUGH THE NIGHT
BACK AT CAMP, THEIR ABSENTEES
GAVE WILL AND STAR A FRIGHT
IN HIS PICK-UP TRUCK, THEY MIGHT HAVE LUCK
AS THEY VENTURED OUT OF SIGHT
FOR CO-CO-MO AND WHITE HORSE
HAD VANISHED IN THE NIGHT

AS I WATCHED THE DUST, FROM HIS PICK-UP
TRUCK
SETTLE TO THE GROUND
I STAYED IN CAMP, T'WAS COLD AND DAMP
AND THE FOREST MADE NO SOUND
AND THE COFFEE SMELL, WAS RICH AND GOOD
THAT IT TURNED MY HEAD AROUND
SO I CALLED OUT TO THE STALLIONS
BUT THE STALLIONS MADE NO SOUND

WELL CO-CO-MO AND WHITE HORSE
WERE WILD AS THE WIND
BUT IN THE WOODS, A COUGAR
IS NOT A HORSE'S FRIEND
IN A FOREST DENSE, THEIR COMMON SENSE
WOULD SAVE THEM IN THE END
AS CO-CO-MO AND WHITE HORSE
GRAZED A FAR OFF GLEN

WELL WILL AND STAR DROVE BACK TO CAMP
NO SMILES ON THEIR FACE
THE GLOOM AND DOOM WAS HEAVY
SO WILL TOOK UP THE CHASE
HE GRABBED A ROPE AND BEGAN HIS LOPE
WITH THREE-SOCKS STEADY PACE
THE DOG AHEAD, PICKED UP THEIR SCENT
AS WILL BEGAN THE RACE

WHILE BACK AT CAMP, THE STAR AND I
BEGAN TO BREAK DOWN CAMP
WAY OUT IN THE MEADOW LANDS
THE AIR WAS COOL AND DAMP
AND IN A WHILE, STAR CRACKED A SMILE
AND LIT UP LIKE A LAMP
AS WILL LED BOTH TO SAFETY
THE SAFETY OF OUR CAMP

WELL CO-CO-MO AND WHITE HORSE
SHONE BRILLIANT IN THE SUN
NEAR OUR CAMP, THEY RAN AND PLAYED
AND HAD A LOT OF FUN
AND STAR AND WILL, COULDN'T GET THEIR FILL
OF THE WILDNESS OF THE TWO
AND THE BEAUTY OF THESE STALLIONS
AND THE NATURAL BEAUTY TOO

# LIGHT OUR LIGHT


THE RIGHT WINGS GOT BLACK FIGHTING WHITE
IT TRIES TO TURN PEACE INTO FIGHT
THE C.I.A.'S TURNING WRONG INTO RIGHT
WITH CRIPS AND BLOODS AT THEIR HEIGHT
WITH HARD DRUGS POURING IN LIKE A BLIGHT
WHILE SKIN HEADS WANT TO KILL AND FIGHT
DOES IT MAKE YOU WANT SOME LIGHT
TO TURN ON OUR LOVE, TO MAKE LIFE RIGHT

WELL I THINK WE CAN BEAT THEM FOREVER
LIGHT YOUR LIGHT AND SEE US TOGETHER
DO WHAT'S RIGHT AND SAY WE'LL NEVER
SELL OUT.....NO NEVER SELL OUT

STAY ON TRACK, WE'LL ALL GET THERE
TRY TO LOVE, TRY TO SHARE
TRY THE DOVE, AND THEN TO DARE
TO DARE TO LOVE, TO DARE TO CARE

AND I KNOW WE CAN, MAKE IT TOGETHER
LIGHT YOUR LIGHT AND SHINE IT FOREVER
AIM YOUR SIGHT AND SAY WE'D BETTER
LIVE RIGHT.....YES EVER SO RIGHT
DAY AND NIGHT, WE'LL LIGHT UP OUR LIGHT
DAY AND NIGHT, WE'LL ALL SEE THE LIGHT
THROUGH THIS LIGHT, WE'LL ALWAYS SHINE
BRIGHT

# MELANCHOLY BAY

WHEN I WAS A YOUNG MAN, ON SAN FRANCISCO
BAY
I'D WALK UPON THE MOUNTAINS, ON A BRIGHT
AND SUNNY DAY
I'D GAZE DOWN TO THE VALLEY, SANTA CLARA
WAS ITS NAME
AND GAZE OUT IN THE SPRINGTIME, WHEN ALL
THE BLOSSOMS CAME

OH..SANTA CLARA, ON SAN FRANCISCO BAY
MY HEART YEARNS FOR FEELINGS, FOR THE
TIMES OF YESTERDAY
WHEN…SANTA CLARA, BLOSSOMED IN THE
SPRING
FROM MOUNTAIN, TO MOUNTAIN, MY HEART
WOULD CLEARLY SING

SAN FRANCISCO, SANTA CLARA, MY HEART WILL
ALWAYS LONG
FOR THE BAY OF SAN FRANCISCO, WHOSE
WAVES SING OUT A SONG
THAT CALL OUT TO MY FEELINGS, A CALL BOTH
SAD AND STRONG
TO THE BAYS YESTERDAYS, I BELONG

SAN FRANCISCO…SAN FRANCISCO AND THE
BEAUTY OF THE BAY
SANTA CLARA…SANTA CLARA, SEEMS SO FAR
AWAY
AND MY LONGING FOR ITS BEAUTY, OF SCENES
OF YESTERDAY
WILL LINGER…IN MY HEART…EVERYDAY

SAN FRANCISCO…SAN FRANCISCO, YOUR
GOLDEN GATE CALLS OUT
SANTA CLARA…SANTA CLARA, IN MY HEART
THERE IS NO DOUBT
FOR MY LOVE OF SAN FRANCISCO AND SANTA
CLARA DAYS
AND THE BEAUTY…OF MY MEMORIES…OF THE
BAY
AND THE BEAUTY OF THE BLOSSOMS…BY THE
BAY
OH THE BEAUTY OF THE CITY'S…YESTERDAYS

# FAITH

WHAT WE ALL WANT TO SEE
IS FOR LOVE TO COME ALIVE
WHAT WE ALL WANT TO KNOW
IS THAT LOVE IS STILL ALIVE
WHAT WE ALL NEED TO GIVE
IS THAT LOVE WHICH IS INSIDE
WHAT WE ALL WANT TO FEEL
IS THAT LOVE IS STILL ALIVE


AND WHEN I'M HERE
I WANT TO BE THERE
AND WHEN I'M THERE
I WANT TO BE SOMEWHERE ELSE SOON


SO AS I TRAVEL HERE
AND I TRAVEL THERE
I SEEM TO LOSE ALL OF MY CARES


AS I TRAVEL WITH THE LIGHT, OF THE SILVERY
MOON
I KNOW THAT I'LL REACH
MY DESTINY SOON


FAITH, IS BELIEVING THAT MAN CAN BE GOOD!

# LIVE RIGHT NOW

YOU LOVE ME
AND I LOVE YOU
SO LOVE YOUR NEIGHBOR
IT SHOULD'T BE A WORK OF LABOR

MUSIC ART AND FORM
MUST RISE THROUGH THIS STORM

SO LOVE YOUR NEIGHBOR
IT SHOULD BE A HIGH TO SAVOR

FATHERS, MOTHERS, DAUGHTERS TOO
FRIENDS, SISTERS, BROTHERS TOO

WILD CREATURES, SEAS SO BLUE
TREES, RIVERS, EARTH SO TRUE

JUST LIVE TO LOVE
YES, LOVE TO LIVE
JUST GIVE TO LOVE
AND LOVE YOURSELF
AND LOVE YOURSELF
AND LOVE YOURSELF
AND LIVE RIGHT NOW
AND LIVE RIGHT NOW
AND LIVE RIGHT NOW!

# RIDE ON

SAVE OUR CHILDREN, SAVE OUR FORESTS
SAVE OUR OCEANS AND OUR BLUE SKY
SAVE OUR RIVERS, SAVE OUR LAKES
SAVE OUR CREATURES, FOR YOU AND I

FOR OUR FUTURE, FOR OUR CHILDREN
FOR OUR PLANET AND OUR SOULS
FOR OUR HEARTS, FOR OUR MINDS
FOR OUR SPIRIT, TO BECOME WHOLE

IT'S OUR DUTY, IT'S OUR PLEASURE
IT'S OUR JOY AND OUR MIRTH
IT'S OUR FREEDOM, IT'S OUR GOAL
IT'S OUR WAY, TO GAIN REBIRTH

AND IT WILL SAVE US, FOR ALL TOMORROWS
TO SHINE THE LIGHT, UPON OUR SOULS
AND IT WILL GIVE US, HOPE FOR TOMORROW
AND SHINE THE WAY, TO REACH OUR GOALS

FOR LIFE FOREVER AND LOVE FOREVER
TO BE TOGETHER AND MEND OUR SOULS
SO GIVE YOURSELVES, TO ONE ANOTHER
AND GIVE YOUR HEARTS, FOREVER MORE

# YOU

IF ANYONE CAN CHANGE THIS WORLD
IT SURELY CAN BE YOU
IF YOU THINK YOU CAN CHANGE THIS WORLD
YOU WILL AND THAT IS TRUE
IF YOU THINK YOU CAN'T, YOU WON'T
AND ALL YOU'LL BE IS BLUE
IF ANYONE CAN CHANGE THIS WORLD
IT SURELY CAN BE YOU

IF YOU WANT THE WORLD TO LOVE
THEN ALL YOU'VE GOT TO DO
IS BE A SOUL OF LOVE, YOURSELF
YOU'LL FIND IT'S TRIED AND TRUE
BUT IF YOU DON'T, YOU KNOW YOU WON'T
AND ALL YOU'LL BE IS BLUE
IF ANYONE CAN CHANGE THIS WORLD
IT SURELY CAN BE YOU

IF YOU THINK YOU CAN CHANGE THIS WORLD
YOU WILL AND THAT IS TRUE
SO LIGHTEN UP YOUR HEARTS MY FRIENDS
THIS SIMPLE TRUTH IS DUE
IF ANYONE CAN CHANGE THIS WORLD
I KNOW THAT IT IS YOU
SO GIVE IT ONE MORE CHANCE MY FRIENDS
YOU WILL AND THAT IS TRUE
YOU CAN AND THAT IS TRUE
YOU WILL AND THAT IS TRUE!

# WE

WE…AS BROTHERS AND SISTERS
SHALL NOT FORGET THIS TIE
THIS BOND…WHICH IN THE SIXTIES
WAS OUR CALL AND CRY FOR FREEDOM
OUR CALL FOR PEACE
OUR CALL FOR LOVE
OUR CALL FOR HUMANITY
SO THAT "WE THE PEOPLE"
SHALL NOT SQUANDER THESE BASIC AND
SIMPLE TRUTHS
EVEN UNDER FIRE, FROM THOSE WHO SAY
THAT THIS GOAL IS IMPOSSIBLE, IDEALISTIC
FANTASY…OR MERELY A DREAM
THAT ALL MEN AND WOMEN
REGARDLESS OF FAITH, COLOR OR ORIGIN
CAN AND MUST LIVE TOGETHER
AS BROTHERS AND SISTERS
IN HARMONY…WITH OUR BEAUTIFUL AND
PERFECT
EDEN EARTH

# About the Author

Born August 28, 1948 in Palo Alto, California, I grew up on the San Francisco Bay, where the Santa Clara Valley bloomed from mountain to mountain at the southern end of the bay.  It was called the fruit basket of the world and is now known as the "Silicon Valley".  My political and environmental values were clear, as the valley became a large populated metropolis and a political hotbed in the 60's.  These songs, prose, and poems are reflections from these changes of environment and political atmosphere as well as the natural beauty of the West from 1950 to 2000; ENJOY!

www.ingramcontent.com/pod-product-compliance
Lightning Source LLC
Chambersburg PA
CBHW031314060726
47590CB00003B/1209